DISCARD

DUE DATE

Books
stained
10·19·0J

PUERTO RICANS

in America

PUERTO RICANS

in America

Ronald J. Larsen

Lerner Publications Company • Minneapolis

LIBRARY OF CONGRESS CATALOGING-IN-PUBLICATION DATA

Larsen, Ronald J., 1948-
    Puerto Ricans in America / Ronald J. Larsen. — Rev. ed.
        p.   cm. — (The In America series)
    Includes index.
    Summary: A brief history of Puerto Rico, Puerto Rican
immigration to the mainland, and the individual contributions
of Puerto Ricans to American life and culture.
    ISBN 0-8225-0238-0 (lib. bdg.)
    ISBN 0-8225-1036-7 (pbk.)
    1. Puerto Ricans—United States—Juvenile literature. [1.
Puerto Ricans—United States.] I. Title. II. Series.
E184.P85L37   1989
973'.04687295—dc19   89-2840
                                                   CIP
                                                   AC

Manufactured in the United States of America

3   4   5   6   7   8   9   10   –   P/JR   –   01   00   99   98   97   96   95   94

CONTENTS ⊗⊘⊗⊘⊗⊘⊗⊘⊗⊘⊗⊘⊗⊘⊗

1
THE LAND AND THE PEOPLE OF PUERTO RICO

The Puerto Rican countryside: a "flowering garden of magical beauty"

Crossroads of the Caribbean

The great chain of islands lying between North and South America and separating the Atlantic Ocean from the Caribbean Sea is known as the West Indies. This island chain is divided into three parts: the Bahamas, the Greater Antilles, and the Lesser Antilles. The most important of these groups is the Greater Antilles, which includes the islands of Cuba, Jamaica, Hispaniola (Haiti and the Dominican Republic), and Puerto Rico (PWER-toh REE-koh).

The smallest and easternmost of the Greater Antilles, the island of Puerto Rico is 1,050 miles from Miami, Florida, and 550 miles from Caracas,

6

Venezuela. Called the "Key to the Indies" and the "Crossroads of the Caribbean," Puerto Rico dominates one of the main entrances from the Atlantic Ocean to the Caribbean Sea. The island is bounded on the north by the Atlantic Ocean, and on the south by the Caribbean Sea.

A small rectangular island, Puerto Rico is about 100 miles long and 35 miles wide. Its lush, green countryside and sandy beaches make Puerto Rico one of the most beautiful islands of the West Indies. Blessed with rich soil, a warm climate, and plenty of sunshine and rain, Puerto Rico abounds with tropical flowers and fruit-bearing trees. It is not surprising, then, that the national anthem of Puerto Rico describes the island as a "flowering garden of magical beauty."

The First Inhabitants

The first inhabitants of Puerto Rico were the Taino (TIE-noh), a subgroup of Arawak Indians. These natives of South America first journeyed from Venezuela to Puerto Rico about 2,000 years ago. The Taino named their new home Boriquén (boh-ree-KEN), or "Land of the Valiant One." Because Boriquén was a land of plenty, the

Puerto Rico:
"Crossroads of the Caribbean"

7

Taino Indians enjoyed a comfortable, easygoing existence there. While the men spent their time fishing and hunting, the women gathered berries, pineapples, and other tropical fruits. The Taino also farmed on a limited basis, planting corn, peanuts, sweet potatoes, and a number of other crops.

The small tribal villages of the Taino were usually located in the valleys, close to the agricultural fields. Most of the villages consisted of simple huts built on either side of a dirt road. The largest hut always belonged to the *cacique* (KAH-see-kay), or chief. The cacique governed all tribal affairs, and his word was law.

The Taino Indians believed that spirits and gods controlled everything in nature, including plants and animals, the earth and the sky, the sun and the rain. In order to please these gods, the Taino honored them with sacred rites and offerings. One god

A hurricane batters the Puerto Rican coast. **Huracán,** *the god of evil, was one god that the Taino Indians could not appease.*

that the Taino could not please, however, was *Huracán* (oo-rah-KAHN), the god of evil. Feared and hated more than any other deity, Huracán brought terrible winds to the island every fall. Today, these winds are called hurricanes.

Although not as grave a threat as Huracán, the fierce Carib Indians who inhabited the islands to the south and east of Boriquén were also feared by the Taino. The Caribs were a bold, seafaring people, and they attacked Boriquén frequently, taking many captives. While the more fortunate captives were enslaved by the Caribs, the less fortunate ones were eaten by them. The Taino Indians were not fond of warfare, but they soon learned to protect themselves from the cannibals whose name was given to the Caribbean Sea.

A Colony of Spain

On September 23, 1493, Christopher Columbus left Spain and set out on his second voyage to the New World. Commanding a fleet of 17 ships, Columbus set his course for Hispaniola, the West Indies island he had explored on his first voyage. Early in November, Columbus stopped at the small Caribbean island of Guadeloupe for water. While exploring the island, he met several Taino Indians who had been taken from the neighboring island of Boriquén and enslaved by the Carib Indians. The Taino begged Columbus to take them home to Boriquén, and Columbus agreed.

The Spanish fleet reached the beautiful green island of Boriquén on November 19, 1493. Impressed with the island, Columbus took possession of it in the name of Ferdinand and Isabella, the rulers of Spain. He named the island San Juan Bautista, after Saint John the Baptist. After a three-day stop at the island, Columbus and his fleet left to continue their voyage to Hispaniola.

For 15 years, the island of San Juan Bautista was ignored by Spain. But in 1508, a Spanish nobleman, Ponce de León, was sent with 50 men to explore the island. On the north coast of the island, Ponce de León discovered a large, well-protected bay. Upon viewing the bay, he exclaimed, "Ay, que puerto rico!" ("Oh, what a rich port!"). In time, the whole island became known as Puerto Rico, while the port itself became known as San Juan—a shortened version of the island's former name.

When Ponce de León and his men landed on the island, they were received well by the friendly Taino Indians. In their bright armor and glittering helmets, the Spaniards seemed like gods to the Indians. As a gesture of friendship and peace, the great Taino chief Agüeybana exchanged names with Ponce de León, thereby making the Spaniard his son. But Ponce de León and his men were more

interested in the chief's gold necklace than in his friendship. When they asked him where the gold came from, the chief told them that the streams of the Yauco River were rich with it. After visiting the streams, the Spaniards could hardly contain their delight at finding gold.

In 1509 Ponce de León began the first Spanish settlement in Puerto Rico. That same year he was made the first governor of the island. Believing the Spaniards to be gods sent from the land of immortals, the Taino peacefully submitted to their authority. Taking advantage of the Indians' peaceful nature, the Spaniards enslaved them and seized their lands. In return for laboring in the gold mines

Above: *Ponce de León.* **Right:** *Forced into slavery by the Spaniards, many Tainos died of exhaustion and disease.*

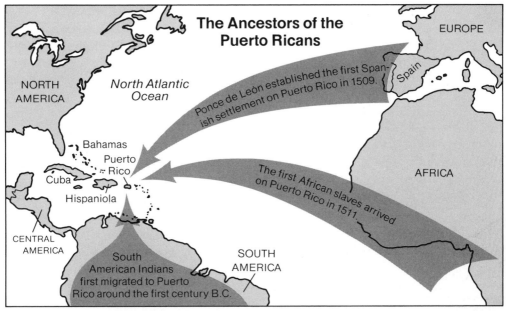

The Ancestors of the Puerto Ricans

NORTH AMERICA

North Atlantic Ocean

EUROPE

Spain

Ponce de León established the first Spanish settlement on Puerto Rico in 1509.

Bahamas

Puerto Rico

Cuba

Hispaniola

AFRICA

The first African slaves arrived on Puerto Rico in 1511.

CENTRAL AMERICA

South American Indians first migrated to Puerto Rico around the first century B.C.

SOUTH AMERICA

Puerto Rico's citizens are descended from the Indians, Spaniards, and Africans who settled the island.

and farms of their Spanish masters, the Taino were offered instruction in the Christian faith and the Spanish culture.

The Taino soon regretted their peaceful submission to the Spaniards. They saw some of their captors die, so they no longer looked upon them as gods. Forced to labor in the mines and fields, many of the Indians died of exhaustion and mistreatment. Others died of diseases brought to the island by the Spaniards. In 1511, after their pleas for better treatment were ignored, the Indians rebelled. Enraged, Ponce de León and 120 Spanish soldiers shot more than 6,000 of the natives. Many of the Indians who were

not killed fled to the mountains and to the neighboring islands.

Convinced that the Taino Indians were useless as workers, Ponce de León begged Ferdinand V, king of Spain, for permission to bring African slaves to Puerto Rico. Permission was granted, and in 1511 the first shipload of black slaves arrived at the island. With the slaves came a terrible epidemic of smallpox that wiped out more than one-third of the dwindling Taino population. By 1515 fewer than 4,000 of the original 40,000 Taino Indians remained on the island. Their numbers were further reduced by another plague in 1519. The few remaining Taino slaves, and those Indians

Caca Fogo. *Caca Plata.*

Spanish ships carrying the gold and silver of the New World were frequently threatened by French, Dutch, and English fleets.

who survived in the mountains and on neighboring islands eventually intermarried with the Spaniards and Africans.

By the 1530s, Puerto Rico had been stripped of nearly all its gold. As a result, the Spaniards turned to agriculture for their livelihood. Sugarcane, which had been brought to Puerto Rico from Hispaniola in 1515, soon became the island's most important crop. In time, a number of small sugar mills were operating on the island.

Although sugarcane offered Puerto Rico some hope of economic survival, the island was beset with problems throughout the 16th century. The African slaves were resentful of the harsh treatment they received and attempted many unsuccessful rebellions. In addition to the slave uprisings, the island was plagued with devastating hurricanes, serious outbreaks of smallpox and other diseases, frequent raids by the Carib Indians, and numerous attacks by French, Dutch, and English pirates.

Spain recognized the strategic importance of Puerto Rico as the gateway to the West Indies and began converting the island into a military outpost during the 16th century. Spain was particularly eager to protect the port of San Juan because Spanish ships carrying the gold of Peru and the silver of Mexico frequently stopped there for supplies and repairs. So in 1533, work began on San Juan's first fortress, La Fortaleza. Six years later, Spain

El Morro's towering walls guard the entrance to San Juan Harbor. The massive fort was one of the Spanish empire's principal bastions in the New World.

began to build El Morro, the largest fortress in San Juan. Situated on the rocky tip of land overlooking the narrow entrance to the harbor, El Morro was built with towering 140-foot walls. Since the powerful guns of the fortress could be pointed at every approach to the harbor, Spain was confident of San Juan's ability to protect itself. But just to make sure, Spain installed a permanent military installation at El Morro in 1586.

El Morro's first important test came in 1595. That year Sir Francis Drake attacked San Juan in an attempt to win it for England. But El Morro's mighty guns blasted the English ships, killing more than 500 of Drake's men. After three days of fighting, Drake and his fleet fled the island in defeat. Three years later, San Juan was attacked by another Englishman—George Clifford, the earl of Cumberland. Rather than attempt to land at San Juan's well-protected harbor, Clifford landed his fleet at a spot several miles to the east.

With 1,000 troops, Clifford marched to San Juan, forced the surrender of El Morro, and captured the city. But five months later, a terrible epidemic of dysentery drove Clifford and his men from the island, and they never returned.

In 1625 Puerto Rico almost fell to the Dutch. With an expedition of 17 ships and 2,500 men, Captain Bowdoin Hendrik sailed directly into San Juan Harbor and took possession of the city. But after three weeks of fighting, the Dutch forces still had not won control of El Morro. Hendrik told the Spaniards he would burn San Juan to the ground if they did not surrender the fortress. When the Spaniards responded by continuing their attack on the Dutch, Hendrik set fire to the city and departed. El Morro was left undefeated, but San Juan lay in ruins.

In order to prevent anyone from ever capturing San Juan again, Spain decided to build a huge wall around the city. Finished in the 1650s, the massive wall was 25 feet high and 18 feet thick. Since it was guarded by three fortresses (El Morro foremost among them), the great wall of San Juan made the city almost unconquerable.

With the exception of Hendrik's attack in 1625, the 17th century was a relatively peaceful period in Puerto Rico's history. Since Spain was more concerned with the island's military role than with its economy, it did not establish huge plantations requiring slave labor on Puerto Rico. As a result,

Unable to conquer El Morro, Dutch forces leave San Juan Harbor.

The great wall surrounding San Juan was completed in the 1650s. In the late 1800s, portions of the wall were demolished to allow easier access to the city.

Puerto Rico was one of the few islands in the Caribbean on which the white population far outnumbered the black slaves. And since the Spaniards had learned to treat their African slaves better than they had treated the Taino, the slaves no longer rebelled against them. In fact, slaves were treated so much better in Puerto Rico that many runaway slaves from British colonies in the Caribbean came to the island to seek refuge. Not wishing to enslave those asking for his protection, the king of Spain declared the runaway slaves free persons.

By the end of the 17th century, many Puerto Rican people were a mixture of three racial-cultural groups: Native American, Spanish, and African. It was from the mixture of these three diverse groups that the Puerto Rican people gradually evolved. In San Juan, where intermarriage had always been widespread (partly because of the shortage of Spanish women), Spanish-Indian and Spanish-African people were becoming quite common.

Until the 19th century, Puerto Rico was forbidden by royal decree to trade with any country except Spain. The only place where the ban was actually enforced, however, was San Juan. In the more remote areas along the island's coast, farmers secretly traded with French, Dutch, and English ships. This illegal trade continued throughout the 17th and 18th centuries.

During the 18th century, Puerto Rico was allowed to export more goods to Spain than ever before. This stimulated agricultural production on the island. Coffee, which was introduced to Puerto Rico in 1736, soon became the island's most important crop. Sugar and tobacco—the traditional crops of Puerto Rico—were raised on a much larger scale than in the past. Although this great expansion in

Tobacco, a traditional crop of Puerto Rico, is handpicked on a hillside farm.

Puerto Rico's agricultural production brought more slaves to the island, the slaves were never more than 10 percent of the island's population.

The agricultural boom in Puerto Rico strengthened the island's economy and stimulated a rapid growth in its population. The population rose from 45,000 in 1765 to 103,000 in 1787 and to 150,000 in 1800. (Of the 150,000 people living in Puerto Rico in 1800, 50 percent were Spanish, 30 percent were of mixed blood, 10 percent were free blacks, and 10 percent were enslaved blacks.) As Puerto Rico's population grew, the island gained a number of new towns. In 1690 the island had only five towns; by 1800 it claimed more than 30.

With the close of the 18th century came the last major English attack on San Juan. In 1796 Spain and France jointly declared war on their common foe, England. In response, England sent a fleet of 60 ships to invade the Caribbean and to capture Spain's colonies. Since England had recently lost its American colonies, it needed to win control of Spain's holdings in the New World to retain its status as a world power.

Under the command of General Ralph Abercromby, the English fleet captured the island of Trinidad with very little effort. The victorious English fleet headed for Puerto Rico in April 1797. Since San Juan was now protected by a great wall and several fortresses, Abercromby landed to the east of the city just as George Clifford had done 100 years earlier. The Puerto Ricans were determined to defend their city from the English, and they gathered a fighting force of more than 6,500 men. Even *jíbaros* (HEE-bah-ros), or farmers, came down from the hills to defend San Juan. Although Abercromby had more than 7,000 troops, he was unable to break the defenses of the Puerto Ricans. After a month of unsuccessful attacks on San Juan, the English fleet left Puerto Rico in defeat.

Toward Autonomy

The 19th century was a period of great political unrest for Puerto Rico. During the three previous centuries, the island had been ruled by a Spanish governor whose authority was absolute. All high government posts, in fact, had been filled by Spaniards. The native Puerto Ricans had virtually no political rights, and the only country they were permitted to trade with was Spain.

With the opening of the 19th century, the people of Puerto Rico began to clamor for greater freedom. Unfortunately, Spain was too involved with its own political problems to deal effectively with those of Puerto Rico. The Spanish government underwent several upheavals during the 19th century, moving from monarchy to republic and back again to monarchy.

As a result, its policies regarding Puerto Rico swung back and forth like a pendulum. Over and over again, Puerto Rico was invited to send representatives to the Spanish *Cortes*, or parliament. Each time, Spain promised reforms that would give Puerto Rico greater freedom and control over its own affairs. And each time, Spain failed to keep its promises. Although Puerto Rico did enjoy some very brief periods of increased political freedom, these periods were followed by long stretches of absolute rule by Spanish governors. To the Puerto Ricans, it seemed as if their island was destined to remain a tightly controlled colony of Spain forever.

Puerto Rico's only major step forward during the first half of the 19th century was in the area of foreign trade. In 1810 Ramón Power, acting as Puerto Rico's first representative to the Spanish Cortes, strongly attacked Spain's rigid trade policies. Five years later, in 1815, King Ferdinand VII issued the *Cédula de Gracias*, or Decree of Grace. Among other things, this important decree opened Puerto Rico's ports to the commerce of all nations. The long-awaited decree brought about the growth of both the economy and the population of Puerto Rico (by 1900, the island's population had risen to almost one million).

Fifty years after the Decree of Grace was passed, Puerto Rico's pleas for greater political freedom and independence had still not been answered.

Tired of waiting for Spain to act, a radical group of Puerto Ricans decided to take matters into their own hands. The leader of the group, Ramón Emeterio Betances, felt that the time had come to declare Puerto Rico's independence from Spain. So, on September 23, 1868, he and 400 armed followers marched into the small mountain town of Lares and captured the town hall. Raising banners with the words "Liberty or Death!" Ramón Emeterio[1] and his men proclaimed the birth of the Republic of Puerto Rico. Called *El Grito de Lares* ("The Cry of Lares"), the one-day uprising did not have popular support and was quickly put down. Its flag, however, was later adopted as the official flag of Puerto Rico.

In the years following the unsuccessful armed revolution of 1868, a strong movement for self-government arose in Puerto Rico. Spain abolished slavery in 1873, but this reform was not enough to satisfy Puerto Rican liberals, who longed for control over their own commerce, industry, education, and government. So in 1887, a group of liberals held a peaceful assembly of protest at the city of Ponce. Although the assembly declared its loyalty to Spain, it demanded

self-rule for Puerto Rico.

In response to the assembly, the Spanish governor of Puerto Rico began a reign of terror in which all known liberals were hunted down and imprisoned. Instead of dissolving Puerto Rico's movement for self-government, these violent attacks strengthened the movement. Within months of the 1887

Luis Muñoz Rivera

[1]*It is a Spanish tradition for children to use both their father's and mother's last names, in that order. But when only one surname is used, it is always the father's. Hence Ramon Emeterio Betances would be called Ramon Emeterio or Emeterio Betances, but never Ramon Betances.*

assembly, the Partido Unionista, or Autonomy Party, was formed. As its name indicated, the object of this party was to secure political autonomy, or self-rule, for Puerto Rico.

In 1891, Luis Muñoz Rivera became the leader of the Autonomy Party. While some Puerto Ricans wanted to revolt against Spain and win complete independence, Muñoz Rivera believed that the island should remain a Spanish territory. But he wanted to secure self-rule for the island through peaceful, nonviolent means. When Cuba—Spain's only remaining colony in the New World besides Puerto Rico—revolted in 1895, Muñoz Rivera feared that Puerto Rico might take a similar course of action. So in 1896 he went to Spain to urge a grant of autonomy for the island. Práxedes Sagasta, the head of Spain's Liberal Party, promised that when his party gained control in Spain, Puerto Rico would be granted self-rule.

When the Liberal Party came to power in 1897, Sagasta became prime minister of Spain. Just as he had promised, Sagasta granted Puerto Rico a Charter of Autonomy. In addition to giving Puerto Rico representation in the Spanish Cortes, the charter allowed the Puerto Ricans to elect most of their own government officials. More importantly, it gave Puerto Rico a two-chamber parliament, which consisted of a Chamber of Representatives and a Council of Administration. When a six-man executive cabinet was formed in Puerto Rico, Luis Muñoz Rivera was chosen as its leader. Since Muñoz Rivera was the first leader of the Puerto Rican government, he is often called the George Washington of Puerto Rico.

Unfortunately, self-rule did not last long in Puerto Rico. Less than a year after the Charter of Autonomy was granted, the island fell under the

The executive cabinet of Puerto Rico's brief autonomous government of 1897. **Seated, left to right:** *Luis Muñoz Rivera, Francisco Quiñones, Manuel Fernandez Juncos.* **Standing, left to right:** *Juan Hernandez Lopez, José Sepero Quiñones, Manuel F. Rossy*

General Nelson A. Miles

control of a country even more powerful than Spain. So ended 400 years of Spanish domination, and so ended Puerto Rico's hard-won right to govern itself.

A U.S. Possession

When Cuba began its final revolt against Spain in 1895, most Americans sympathized with its cause. So in 1898, when it became clear that Cuba needed help to win its independence, the United States intervened and declared war on Spain. After freeing Cuba from Spanish control in July 1898, American forces headed for Puerto Rico. On July 25, 1898, General Nelson A. Miles landed on the southwest coast of the island with a force of 3,500 men. Because most Puerto Ricans hoped that the United States would ensure democracy and prosperity for their island, they put up very little opposition to the invasion.

On October 18, 1898, President William McKinley made General John R. Brooke the first American military governor of Puerto Rico. With Brooke's installation as the new governor of Puerto Rico, Spain's flag at El Morro was replaced by the Stars and Stripes. Having lost the Spanish-American War, Spain signed the Treaty of Paris on December 10, 1898, and officially ceded Puerto Rico to the United States.

The military government established on the island lasted until 1900.

General John R. Brooke

Although it deprived the Puerto Ricans of self-rule, it nevertheless improved the island's sanitation facilities, established an educational system, and built many highways, railroads, hospitals, and other public works. By and large, the two-year period of military government was a peaceful and productive time in Puerto Rico's history. The Puerto Ricans did suffer one insult during this period, however. Their island was mistakenly called "Porto" Rico on all official U.S. documents, and the error continued well into the 1930s.

In 1900 the U.S. Congress gave Puerto Rico some measure of self-rule by passing the first Organic Act, or the Foraker Act. This act replaced the island's military government with a two-house civil government. While the U.S. president retained the right to appoint the governor, his cabinet, and the upper legislative body, the Puerto Ricans were allowed to elect the lower legislature, as well as a resident commissioner in Washington, D.C. The resident commissioner could speak to the U.S. Congress on Puerto Rican affairs, but he had no vote. The Foraker Act did not give U.S. citizenship to Puerto Ricans, and it did not require them to pay federal taxes. It did establish free trade between the island and the United States—a significant advantage for Puerto Rico.

The Foraker Act gave Puerto Rico a civil government, but it left the island's political status in serious doubt. Puerto Rico was not an independent nation, nor a colony, nor a autonomous commonwealth, nor a state in the American union. The Foraker Act specified only that Puerto Rico was a U.S. possession—nothing more and nothing less.

Dissatisfied with Puerto Rico's uncertain status under the Foraker Act, Luis Muñoz Rivera went to Washington, D.C., in 1910 as the resident commissioner of his island. Accompanying Muñoz Rivera was his 12-year-old son, who one day would carry on his father's work. After arriving in Washington, Muñoz Rivera began his long crusade to win from the United States what he had won from Spain more than 10 years earlier—autonomy for Puerto Rico. His tireless struggle paid off, for in 1917, the U.S. Congress passed the second Organic Act, or the Jones Act. This act defined Puerto Rico as an "organized but unincorporated" territory of the United States and made the Puerto Ricans citizens of the United States. Although it maintained the right of the U.S. president to appoint the governor of Puerto Rico, it gave the islanders the right to elect *both* houses of their government. The Jones Act did not give autonomy to Puerto Rico, but it was nevertheless a triumph for the island and for the island's greatest crusader—Luis Muñoz Rivera. Unfortunately, this great patriot died before the Jones Act could be put into effect.

From 1900 to 1925, the advancement of Puerto Rico's economy paralleled that of the island's political status. This period of great economic expansion in Puerto Rico was due partly to the increased trade with the United States and partly to U.S. government funding for roads, dams, hospitals, and schools on the island. But more important to the island's economy were U.S. businesses. Since the island was a territory of the United States, no duty, or tax, had to be paid on exports and imports moving back and forth between Puerto Rico and the United States. Encouraged by this protection, many American manufacturers moved their businesses to the island. In a move that would have even greater impact, American businesses invested in Puerto Rico's rich agricultural land, buying up small sugar fields from jíbaros and consolidating them into a few giant corporations.

Soaring sugar production gave the Puerto Rican economy a dramatic boost. Reflecting the expanding economy was an expanding population. Between 1900 and 1925, the population rose from about one million people to well over two million. By 1925, Puerto Rico's fantastic birth rate was quickly making the island one of the most densely populated areas in the entire world.

Jíbaros who toiled in the sugar fields benefited very little from soaring sugar production in the early 20th century.

Sugar mills on Puerto Rico. Profits went to the large corporations and investors on the U.S. mainland.

Unfortunately, the economic expansion in Puerto Rico did not benefit the working people of the island. American sugar corporations continued to make tremendous profits, but these profits went to the wealthy investors from the United States—*not* to the poor Puerto Rican jíbaros who worked long hours in the fields and mills. On the whole, the jíbaros were paid very low wages—sometimes less than 50 cents a day. And since the work was seasonal (the "dead season" stretched from June to November, while the cane was growing), many Puerto Ricans were out of work for long periods of time. Thus, by converting Puerto Rico's economy into virtually a one-crop economy, American businessmen made the vast majority of Puerto Ricans dependent on an industry that could only employ them on a part-time basis.

Two devastating hurricanes—one in 1928 and one in 1930—left the island's economy in an even worse state than before. While the American-owned sugar corporations continued to make money, the working-class people of Puerto Rico fell further into poverty. The unemployment and infant mortality rates increased greatly, and the

Substandard housing was just one of many problems that plagued Puerto Rico during the Great Depression.

islanders contended with hunger, poor housing, and disease. As the terrible depression years of the 1930s descended upon the island (and upon the entire United States), Puerto Rico's poverty-stricken state earned the island yet another name: the "Poorhouse of the Caribbean."

When President Franklin Roosevelt came to office in 1933, he set up relief and reconstruction agencies for Puerto Rico that were similar to the agencies that were helping depression victims on the mainland. The Puerto Ricans were U.S. citizens, after all, and they desperately needed the government's help. So in 1933, Roosevelt established the Puerto Rico Emergency Relief Administration, or PRERA. During its two-year life, this organization spent millions of dollars on food, clothing, and job training programs for the Puerto Ricans. In a very real way, PRERA kept Puerto Ricans alive.

In 1935 Roosevelt established another organization to aid the islanders—the Puerto Rico Reconstruction Administration, or PRRA. This organization was aimed primarily at establishing new industries in Puerto Rico so that the island's economy would not be solely dependent upon agriculture. In addition to starting shoe and garment industries on the island, PRRA gave Puerto Rican farmers the right to buy back their land from one of the island's four giant sugar corporations.

Shortly after the creation of PRRA, Luis Muñoz Marín, the son of patriot Luis Muñoz Rivera, emerged as Puerto Rico's newest and most dynamic political leader. In 1938 he and his followers formed a progressive new party called Partido Popular Democratico (Popular Democratic Party), or PPD. As the 1940 legislative elections in Puerto Rico neared, Muñoz Marín claimed that the political status of the island was not the real issue of the election. Rather, the state of the island's economy was the issue. With "Bread, Land, and Liberty" as its slogan, the PPD proposed sweeping economic and social reforms for the island. Muñoz Marín's appeal to the working classes proved successful, for the Popular Democratic Party succeeded in winning a slim majority in Puerto Rico's legislature.

Luis Muñoz Marín, campaigning under the banner of the Popular Democratic Party, proposed sweeping economic and social reform for Puerto Rico.

"Bread, Land, Liberty"–*the motto of the Popular Democratic Party.*

Following his party's victory, Muñoz Marín initiated the miraculous economic development program that was eventually to lift Puerto Rico out of poverty. Called "Operation Bootstrap," the progressive program received extensive financial backing from the U.S. government. "Operation Bootstrap" aimed to develop business and industry on the island, improve health care and education, clear slum areas, provide new housing, increase agricultural production, and redistribute land to the jíbaros by breaking up the large sugar corporations. Although it took many years, millions of dollars, and a lot of hard work to achieve these goals, they all were eventually realized.

Impressed with the economic and social reforms begun under Operation Bootstrap, the Puerto Ricans gave overwhelming support to Muñoz Marín and the Popular Democratic Party in the 1944 legislative elections. Three years later, the U.S. Congress passed a law that paved the way for an even greater victory for Muñoz Marín. In an amendment to the Jones Act, Congress at last gave the people of Puerto Rico the right to elect their own governor. When the 1948 elections were held in Puerto Rico, Luis Muñoz Marín became the first governor of Puerto Rico to be elected by the Puerto Rican people. January 2, 1949, the day of Muñoz Marín's inauguration, was a proud and historic day for Puerto Rico.

Operation Bootstrap undertook extensive slum clearance and urban renewal. Modern housing projects (below) replaced substandard housing (right).

Following his inauguration, Governor Muñoz devoted himself to making Operation Bootstrap a success. World War II had thwarted the ambitious economic program, leaving Puerto Rico's economy in a very weakened condition. So to realize Operation Bootstrap's main goal of industrialization, Muñoz Marín created Fomento, or the Economic Development Association. Designed to encourage U.S. investors to establish industries in Puerto Rico, the agency was a tremendous success. As more and more businesses and factories were established on the island, Puerto Rico slowly made the transition from an agricultural to an industrial society.

Of course, the startling transformation of the island's economy did not occur overnight. Following World War II and through the 1950s, the economy experienced many growing pains and many setbacks. As a result, thousands of unemployed Puerto Ricans left the island and migrated to the continental United States in the hopes of finding work and making a better life for themselves. During the 1960s, however, as Puerto Rico's economy began to improve, the great Puerto Rican exodus to the mainland ended.

The Commonwealth

In addition to his work on Operation Bootstrap, Governor Muñoz began a campaign to improve Puerto Rico's political status. During the 1940 elections, Muñoz Marín had said that Puerto Rico's economy—*not* its status—was the issue. But in 1949, as progress was being made on the island's economy, Muñoz Marín felt that the time had come for the political status of his homeland to become the issue. The Independent Party favored independence for Puerto Rico, and the State Republican Party favored making the island an American state. But Governor Muñoz and the Popular Democratic Party wanted to make Puerto Rico a self-governing commonwealth of the United States. As such, the Puerto Ricans would govern their island and the United States would defend it. The people of Puerto Rico would remain United States citizens,

Union Carbide's chemical plant near Ponce. Fomento helped transform Puerto Rico from an agricultural to an industrial society.

but they would pay no federal taxes and have no vote in the national government.

On October 30, 1950, President Harry S. Truman paved the way for making Puerto Rico a self-governing commonwealth by signing Public Law 600, which gave the Puerto Ricans the right to draft their own constitution. In August 1951, Puerto Ricans elected 92 delegates to their constitutional convention. Six months later the constitution was completed. Modeled after the U.S. Constitution, it gave Puerto Rico self-government, but stated that the island would remain an associated commonwealth of the United States.

In the elections of 1952, the Puerto Ricans approved the constitution and reelected Muñoz Marín as their governor. Then, on July 25, 1952, the U.S. Congress approved the Puerto Rican Constitution. The Free Associated State of Puerto Rico (Estado Libre Asociado de Puerto Rico), or the Commonwealth of Puerto Rico, as it came to be called, was at last a reality. As Constitution Day was proclaimed throughout the island, a proud Governor Muñoz raised Puerto Rico's flag next to the Stars and Stripes. A new era had begun in the history of Puerto Rico.

In 1964, 12 years after Puerto Rico became a commonwealth, Governor Muñoz announced that he would not seek reelection as governor of the island. He had been elected to the

Roberto Sánchez Vilella

office four times—in 1948, 1952, 1956, and 1960—and he felt it was time to step down. When the 1964 elections were held, Roberto Sánchez Vilella emerged as the island's new governor. Sánchez Vilella had been Muñoz Marín's secretary of state for many years. Luis Muñoz Marín died in 1980.

Although the Popular Democratic Party did well in the 1964 elections, rival parties favoring statehood for Puerto Rico did better than ever before. The movement for Puerto Rican statehood was gaining momentum. As a result, the U.S. Congress appointed a special commission to study Puerto Rico's political status. In 1966, the commission suggested that the Puerto

Luis A. Ferré, a strong advocate of Puerto Rican statehood

Rican people should again vote on their status. When the vote was held on July 23, 1967, the Puerto Ricans had three options: continuation of the commonwealth, statehood, or independence. More than 60 percent of the people voted for the continuation of the commonwealth, with 39 percent wanting statehood and less than 1 percent favoring independence.

The statehood movement failed to win the popular vote, but it showed a surprising amount of strength. And the movement gained even more strength in 1968, when Luis A. Ferré, a strong advocate of statehood, was elected as governor of Puerto Rico. Four years later, however, the statehood movement was all but crushed when Governor Ferré was defeated at the polls by Rafael Hernández Colón, a leader of the Popular Democratic Party and an articulate supporter of the commonwealth. By electing Hernández Colón, and by giving the PPD more than two-thirds of the seats in the legislature, the people of Puerto Rico showed strong support for the continuation of the commonwealth.

Whether Puerto Rico ever becomes a state, its close ties with the United States have led to significant improvements. Through the efforts of Operation Bootstrap, Fomento, and U.S. investors, the island has attracted more than 2,500 factories.

The industrialization achieved through Operation Bootstrap has brought many benefits to the island, including increased employment, higher wages, better housing, and a greatly improved educational system (illiteracy has almost disappeared from the island). All of these improvements have enabled Puerto Rico's 3 million people to achieve a higher standard of living than ever before. One dramatic consequence of the island's improved economy is that Puerto Ricans are now living longer. In the 1930s, before Operation Bootstrap began, the average life span for a Puerto Rican was less than 40 years. In 1985, it had risen to 73.

Although the island faces some serious economic problems in the 1990s, it has already accomplished miracles.

Puerto Rican culture is a mixture of the old and new. **Above:** *Children leave a rural elementary school.* **Below:** *An ancient fort wall juts out in front of a modern cityscape.*

2
THE MIGRATION TO THE U.S. MAINLAND

A group of Puerto Rican women–trained in domestic work–arrive at Newark Airport in New Jersey in 1948.

The First Migrants

Although Puerto Ricans did not begin migrating in large numbers until the 1920s, the Puerto Rican migration to the U.S. mainland actually began around the turn of the century. When Puerto Rico was annexed by the United States in 1898, many islanders lived in great poverty. The overpopulated island was plagued with an underdeveloped economy, massive unemployment, hunger, poor housing, and a high death rate. In search of a better life, small groups of Puerto Ricans journeyed by boat across the Atlantic Ocean.

Merchant seamen, garment makers, college students, and cigar makers were among the first Puerto Ricans to arrive on the U.S. mainland. Although they came in small numbers, their communities gradually grew in size and importance. In 1910, there were about 1,500 Puerto Ricans living on the mainland; by 1920, there were over 7,000 in New York City alone. While most of the migrants settled in New York—the traditional port of entry for boats from Puerto Rico—others settled in Chicago, Boston, New Orleans, and Miami.

With the passage of the Jones Act in 1917, Puerto Rican migration increased dramatically. Since the Jones Act made Puerto Ricans citizens of the United States by birth, the islanders had as much right to move to the U.S. mainland as citizens already living on the mainland had to move from one state to another. Thus, although restrictive immigration laws were passed in the United States in 1921 and 1924, they did not apply to the Puerto Ricans.

When World War I ended in 1918,

Poverty and unemployment on the island prompted many Puerto Ricans to migrate to the mainland in search of a better life.

poverty and unemployment were chronic on Puerto Rico. Laborers had benefited very little from the recent expansion in manufacturing and sugar production on the island. Because of a rising birth rate and a falling death rate, the population of the already overpopulated island was growing faster than ever before. As a result, thousands of Puerto Ricans exercised their rights as U.S. citizens to migrate to the mainland, where the economy was thriving and where jobs were plentiful.

By 1930, more than 53,000 Puerto Ricans were living on the U.S. mainland. Like the first Puerto Ricans who had migrated to the mainland, most of those who came during the 1920s settled in New York City. By 1930, more than 45,000 Puerto Ricans were living in this city. Here, they had no trouble finding work. Since the postwar immigration laws had greatly limited the admission of Europeans to the United States, the Puerto Ricans found many openings in jobs for unskilled and semiskilled workers—jobs that had traditionally been filled by European immigrants. Thousands of Puerto Rican women entered the New York garment industry, while Puerto Rican men found work in factories, hospitals, hotels, restaurants, and laundries.

During the Great Depression, which began in 1929 and lasted well into the 1930s, the migration of the Puerto Ricans to the U.S. mainland slowed down considerably. Jobs were as scarce on the mainland as they were in Puerto Rico, and most Puerto Ricans simply could not afford the price of the boat ticket to the mainland (the cost was more than the average Puerto Rican earned in a year). Yet the Puerto Rican population on the U.S. mainland rose from 53,000 to 70,000 between 1930 and 1940.

The year 1939 saw the beginning of World War II, a war that all but halted Puerto Rican migration to the mainland. Jobs were plentiful in the United States during the war, but submarine warfare in the Caribbean made it difficult and hazardous for Puerto Ricans to make the voyage to the mainland. Some did come, however, and they readily found work.

The Migration Boom

After World War II ended in 1945, the greatest and most important period of the Puerto Rican migration to the continental United States began. Three factors encouraged the exodus of Puerto Ricans to the mainland. First, Puerto Rico's economy was still weak and underdeveloped. Operation Bootstrap had begun in 1940, but its ambitious goals for strengthening the island's economy were far from accomplished. The grave problems of overpopulation, underemployment, and poverty had yet to be solved. Second, a great many jobs for unskilled and semiskilled workers were available on the U.S. mainland. This huge surplus of jobs had been created during the war, when thousands of unskilled laborers in the United States left their jobs to work in defense plants and factories. When the war ended, they continued working in the factories, thereby leaving their former jobs unfilled. And third, air transportation expanded rapidly after the war, becoming an important means of travel. The expansion of commercial air travel meant that large numbers of Puerto Ricans could fly from San Juan to New York City in a matter of hours, and at relatively low costs (some airlines advertised one-way fares as low as $50).

Drawn by the opportunities for employment, thousands upon thousands of Puerto Ricans came to the mainland by plane, thereby beginning the first great airborne migration in history. Although some Puerto Ricans already living on the mainland returned to Puerto Rico, the number of islanders coming to the mainland was far

The textile industry offered employment to many Puerto Rican migrants.

Puerto Rican Migration to the U.S. Mainland
1945 to 1956

1945	13,000	1951	53,000
1946	40,000	1952	59,000
1947	25,000	1953	69,000
1948	33,000	1954	22,000
1949	26,000	1955	45,000
1950	35,000	1956	52,000

greater. In 1945, the net Puerto Rican migration to the continental United States was more than 13,000. The next year, the net migration climbed to almost 40,000. Following the outbreak of the Korean War in 1950, even greater numbers of islanders came to the mainland, primarily because of the increased need for laborers created by the war. In 1953, the year in which the largest number of Puerto Ricans came to the mainland, the net migration was more than 69,000. By 1955, about 675,000 Puerto Ricans were living on the mainland, with 500,000 of them concentrated in New York City.

Toward the end of the 1950s, as automation began reducing the number of jobs for unskilled laborers in the United States, the migration of the Puerto Ricans slowed down markedly. Yet, 900,000 Puerto Ricans were living on the U.S. mainland in 1960. While the vast majority of the migrants were in New York, sizable Puerto Rican communities also developed in New Jersey, Connecticut, Massachusetts, Pennsylvania, Ohio, and Illinois. (The second largest Puerto Rican community on the mainland is in Chicago.) Although some Puerto Rican communities were also established in Florida and California, most Puerto Ricans avoided settling in the South or the West. The South was forbidding because of the racial tension there, and the West was simply too remote for most Puerto Ricans.

The Puerto Ricans living in the East and the Midwest found work in industrial factories, canneries, garment centers, steel mills, and iron foundries. Those employed in the service industries worked as kitchen helpers, bellhops, dishwashers, busboys, and hospital orderlies. Some Puerto Ricans became civil servants (mail-carriers in particular), and others found careers in the armed forces.

Still other Puerto Ricans were employed on the mainland as contract farm workers. When Puerto Rico's sugar season ended in June, thousands of Puerto Rican sugar workers signed contracts with employers to work in the agricultural fields of the northeastern states. In order to protect the migrant workers from unfair treatment, the Commonwealth of Puerto Rico passed laws in 1947 and 1948 stating that the contracts offered by mainland employers had to be approved by Puerto Rico's Department of Labor. About 20,000 Puerto Rican farm workers migrated to the mainland each year. Some of them stayed and became permanent residents. The contract farm worker program is still operating, but the number of workers has declined in recent years.

A Leveling Off

In the 1960s, the Puerto Rican migration to the mainland began to level off, primarily for three reasons. First, jobs on the mainland for unskilled

While some Puerto Rican migrants took jobs in industry (above), others became contract farm workers in the agricultural fields of the northeastern United States (right).

workers, to which the volume of Puerto Rican migration had always been directly related, were becoming increasingly scarce. Second, the goals of Operation Bootstrap were finally being realized in Puerto Rico. As more and more industries were established on the island, unemployment dropped and the standard of living rose. Thus the islanders had less reason to migrate to the mainland.

A third reason for the leveling off of the Puerto Rican migration to the U.S. mainland was the temporary nature of the migration. The European immigrants of earlier years had made the long journey to this country by boat and had come with the intention of staying. Most of the Puerto Ricans, on the other hand, migrated during the aviation age. Airplanes could take them to the U.S. mainland in a matter of hours. Many believed that their real roots were still in Puerto Rico and that one day they would return to the island. While some of these people did eventually return to live in Puerto Rico, others continued to live on the mainland but made frequent trips back to the island. Since the price of an airplane ticket from New York to San Juan was relatively inexpensive, Puerto Ricans could return to their homeland easier than other ethnic groups in the United States could return to theirs.

In the 1960s, there were several years in which more Puerto Ricans returned to the island than came to the mainland. In 1963, for example, 5,000 more Puerto Ricans migrated to the island than to the mainland.

Number of Puerto Ricans on the U.S. Mainland and in New York City

	U.S. MAINLAND	NEW YORK CITY
1910	1,500	500
1920	not available	7,000
1930	53,000	45,000
1940	70,000	61,000
1950	300,000	187,000
1960	900,000	630,000
1970	1,500,000	818,000
1980	2,000,000	861,000
1990	2,728,000	933,000

Whereas European immigrants traveled to the United States by boat in the early 20th century, Puerto Ricans migrating after World War II flew to the mainland by plane in just a few hours.

Nevertheless, the population of the Puerto Ricans on the U.S. mainland increased steadily through the 1960s. The growth in population stemmed not from the arrival of more migrants on the mainland, but rather from the high birth rates of the Puerto Ricans already living there.

During the 10-year period from 1960 to 1970, the Puerto Rican population in the continental United States grew from 900,000 to 1.5 million. In 1990, 2.7 million Puerto Ricans were living on the mainland—about two-thirds as many as were living on the island.

Thousands of Puerto Ricans continue to arrive on the mainland each year. But at the same time, thousands of Puerto Ricans living on the mainland return to the island. Thus the net migration of Puerto Ricans to the mainland is very small. As Puerto Rican families on the mainland (especially in cities such as New York and Chicago) continue to grow in size, however, the Puerto Ricans are becoming an increasingly visible minority in the United States.

3
LIFE ON THE MAINLAND

Men play dominoes, a popular game in Puerto Rico, on the streets of New York.

Land of Plenty

At the end of World War II, thousands of Puerto Ricans made the plane trip from San Juan to New York with the hope of finding a better life on the mainland. As they stepped off the planes at New York City's La Guardia Airport, most of the newcomers carried cardboard suitcases that held everything they owned. Although the migrants were poor, they were confident that in the United States—the land of opportunity—their fortunes would soon change.

Unlike the European immigrants who had come before them, the Puerto Ricans were U.S. citizens before they ever set foot on the mainland. *Like* earlier immigrants, however, they faced the problem of language. Spanish was the official language of Puerto Rico, and very few of the islanders who came to the mainland understood English. Few of those who came during the winter months understood New York's frigid climate either. Snow was something most Puerto Ricans had only seen in movies.

In spite of the language barrier and the cold, the Puerto Rican migrants were glad to be on the mainland. Since they were usually met at the airport by friends and relatives who had come before them, the newcomers felt almost at home. As mentioned earlier, the great majority of the migrants settled in New York City. In most cases, they stayed with relatives until they found work. While they were looking for jobs, they quickly learned to find their way around the towering city they had heard and read so much about. New York was cold and forbidding in many ways, but it was also one of the most exciting cities in the world.

Land of Problems

Between 1945 and the early 1950s, jobs for unskilled and semiskilled laborers were plentiful in the United States—especially in large cities like New York. Thus the Puerto Ricans who came to the mainland during the postwar period had no problems finding work in factories and in the service industries. These jobs provided the migrants with a steady income—something most had never known in Puerto Rico. But at the same time, they were the lowest paying and least desirable jobs in the city.

New York City, with its massive buildings and crowded streets, was often intimidating to the Puerto Rican migrants.

And because most of the Puerto Ricans did not speak or understand English, they had little chance of advancing to higher positions.

At first, the Puerto Ricans were grateful just to be employed, no matter how low their jobs were on the occupational totem pole. After all, they were making higher wages than they had ever made in Puerto Rico. But what they hadn't counted on was the high cost of living in New York. By the time they paid for food, clothing, transportation, and housing, they had little or no money left over. And as U.S. citizens living on the mainland, they were now subject to state and federal taxes—something they didn't face back in Puerto Rico.

Since the Puerto Ricans filled the lowest paying occupations, they had little choice but to live in the poorest neighborhoods. For the Puerto Ricans who settled in New York, this meant living in the inner-city slums. The Puerto Ricans began concentrating in East Harlem, an area on the east side of Manhattan, in the late 1920s. By the late 1940s, so many were living in the area that it became known as Spanish Harlem, or *El Barrio*, which is Spanish for "the Neighborhood." Large

Most Puerto Ricans had little choice but to make their homes in the poorest neighborhoods of New York City.

numbers of Puerto Ricans settled in other areas of the city (notably the East Bronx), but El Barrio was—and still is—the area most strongly identified with New York City's Puerto Rican population.

The housing in El Barrio and other Puerto Rican districts in New York City was overcrowded, high priced, and run down. In many cases, families of seven or more people were crowded into tiny three-room apartments consisting of a combination living room-bedroom, a bathroom, and a kitchen. Less fortunate families lived in a single room, sharing a common bathroom and kitchen with several other families. Whatever the size of the apartment, the conditions were often the same: cracked ceilings and walls, broken windows, faulty plumbing, poor heating, and rats.

Even with both parents working, most Puerto Rican families could not afford better housing. In fact many couldn't even afford to live in the slums. As a result, they turned to city, state, and federal agencies for financial aid. Unlike the immigrants who had come to the United States half a century earlier, the Puerto Ricans who came during and after the 1940s arrived at a time when welfare programs were fairly well established. In this respect, then, they were more fortunate than many of the earlier newcomers.

Poor jobs and poor housing were not the only problems the Puerto Ricans faced on the mainland.

Another serious problem was that of racial prejudice and discrimination. Although thousands of Puerto Ricans had been living in New York City before World War II, they had been relatively unnoticed amid New York's millions of inhabitants. But after the war, as the Puerto Ricans poured into New York and became an increasingly visible minority, the prejudice against them mounted. By the late 1940s, the Puerto Rican migrants were widely known by the derogatory term "spic."

Because of their poor English and their dark skin, the Puerto Ricans were discriminated against in jobs, in housing, and in the more "exclusive" hotels and restaurants. This sort of cruelty based upon color was very difficult for the migrants to understand because they came from a society where racial intermarriage was commonplace and where racial discrimination was practically non-existent.

Color was not an issue in Puerto Rico, but it was a very hot issue on the mainland—especially with blacks beginning their movement for civil rights in the 1950s. Adding fuel to the prejudice against the Puerto Ricans (and the blacks, for that matter) was that many of them had started receiving welfare benefits. This was because many jobs for unskilled laborers, which had been plentiful immediately following the war, were now being eliminated by automation.

Many people on the mainland

On the mainland, many Puerto Rican women took jobs outside of the home for the first time.

accused the Puerto Ricans of migrating solely for the purpose of getting free handouts on the welfare programs. This was a cruel and unjust accusation. In fact, most Puerto Ricans considered it a terrible disgrace to be on welfare. Puerto Rican men and women took great pride in their work.

The dignity and pride of Puerto Rican men living on the mainland was also threatened by the newly elevated position of Puerto Rican women. In Puerto Rico, a woman was expected to stay at home, take care of her children, and bow to the authority of her husband—the unquestioned head of the family. But on the mainland, Puerto Rican women worked outside the home, did the shopping, and dealt with teachers, doctors, and other outside agents.

Because of their strong sense of pride, many Puerto Rican men resented the new freedom and independence of their wives on the mainland. Even more disturbing to them was the fact that their wives often earned more than they did. But the final humiliation came when their wives were working and they were not. Having their wives support them and their families was more than some Puerto Rican men could accept. As a result, they left their families in disgrace. This, in part, explains the high rate of broken marriages among the Puerto Ricans on the mainland during the 1950s.

Other family problems also plagued the Puerto Rican migrants. Since they came from a society where children were expected to respect and obey their parents without question, Puerto Rican adults found it difficult to accept the leniency and freedom granted to children in mainland society. On the other hand, Puerto Rican children enjoyed their new-found freedom on the mainland and rebelled against the attitudes of their parents. This was particularly true of Puerto Rican girls. In Puerto Rico, they had been closely guarded and strictly chaperoned. On the mainland, they ventured outside their homes and engaged in a much freer social life than they had ever known before.

Another thing that broadened the gap between Puerto Rican parents and their children was the fact that in most cases, the children learned English much more rapidly than their parents did. Consequently, Puerto Rican youths adapted to American society quickly and soon abandoned some of the traditions of Puerto Rican culture.

Education was another of the problems faced by the Puerto Ricans who migrated to the mainland. Because most of their teachers spoke only English, Puerto Rican children had a difficult time in school and performed very poorly. Humiliated and discouraged, many dropped out of school and looked for jobs that didn't require much education.

Unable to find work, many of the Puerto Rican youths who had left school banded together into gangs. Although these gangs eventually became involved in violence and bloodshed, they nevertheless served an important and worthwhile purpose. By joining a gang and wearing a jacket with the gang's insignia and name on it, young Puerto Rican men who felt lost and defeated in New York gained a sense of solidarity and toughness. And adding to this sense of toughness was the fact that each gang ruled a special "turf," or territory, of its own.

While most Puerto Rican gangs were at first peaceful, they became more and more warlike as they began to clash with opposing Italian and black gangs. When one gang dared to invade another gang's turf, a "rumble," or fight, erupted. During the 1950s, as the friction between opposing gangs mounted, gang warfare became a serious problem in New York City. (This problem formed the dramatic basis for Leonard Bernstein's stage musical *West Side Story*, which was made into one of the most successful and highly acclaimed motion pictures of the 1960s.

West Side Story *dramatized the racial discrimination encountered by the Puerto Ricans in New York during the 1950s.*

Identity Crisis

Gang fights, lack of education, broken homes, discrimination, unemployment, poor housing, the language barrier—all these were serious problems for the Puerto Ricans on the mainland. But perhaps the most serious problem of all was that of the migrants' *identity*. Since many of the Puerto Ricans living on the mainland still looked upon Puerto Rico as their *real* home, they felt as if they did not

really "belong" to or form a part of the mainland. And this feeling of not belonging was strengthened because as thousands of Puerto Ricans came to the mainland, thousands of others returned home to Puerto Rico.

The identity crisis of the Puerto Ricans was directly linked with the reluctance of the migrants to get involved in mainland politics. As U.S. citizens living on the mainland, the Puerto Ricans had every right to participate in political activities and to vote in political elections. But since many of the migrants were determined to return to Puerto Rico as soon as they had "made good" on the mainland, they did not register to vote or engage in politics. As a result, they had no representatives in the city, state, and federal governments to fight for them or to help improve the quality of their lives on the mainland.

Since the Puerto Ricans did not see themselves as permanent residents of the mainland, they did not establish many community organizations there. Earlier immigrants from Europe had established such organizations to help the immigrants that followed them adjust to life in the United States. But the Puerto Ricans were slow to do so.

Ironically, it was the Puerto Rican government—*not* the Puerto Rican migrants—that established the first important Puerto Rican organizations on the U.S. mainland. In 1948 the Commonwealth of Puerto Rico set up a migration office in New York City in order to help Puerto Ricans living on the mainland. Offices were later established in other cities with large Puerto Rican populations. This was the first time in history that a government crossed an ocean and followed its people to a new land. The aim of the Puerto Rican offices was to make life on the mainland easier for the migrants by helping them find jobs and housing, by offering them free English lessons, and by protecting them against discrimination.

Many Puerto Ricans did not look on the mainland as their home and longed to return to the island.

47

Children play on the streets of El Barrio during the 1940s.

El Barrio

Although the Puerto Rican migrants took little initiative in starting self-help organizations on the mainland, they *did* establish their own communities in New York and other large mainland cities. Of course, the most famous of these was New York's El Barrio. The Neighborhood was distinctly Puerto Rican.

The streets of El Barrio were marked by movie houses showing Spanish-language films, travel agencies offering low-cost flights back to Puerto Rico, and candy stores featuring jukeboxes that played Spanish records. Also part of the Neighborhood were restaurants and bakeries, laundries and clothing shops, dance halls and bars, and *bodegas*—small grocery stores selling fruits, vegetables, and foods imported from Puerto Rico.

Sandwiched in between the many

A busy bodega in the heart of El Barrio

stores of the tightly packed neighborhood were a number of "storefront" churches, most of which were Protestant. Traditionally, most Puerto Ricans were Roman Catholics (Catholicism was brought to Puerto Rico by the Spaniards during the 15th century). On the mainland, however, many Puerto Ricans found the storefront churches established by Protestant sects such as the Baptists and the Pentecostals to be a better source of community and inspiration. These churches had small, tightly knit congregations, and they featured lively services with plenty of singing and clapping. Most important, the churches served a social function for the migrants by sponsoring recreation centers, athletic clubs, and other activities.

During New York's long, cold winter, El Barrio's streets were nearly deserted. Most Puerto Ricans stayed indoors, venturing out into the forbidding cold only for work, school, and shopping. But when summer arrived, the streets of the Neighborhood hummed with activity. Radios, jukeboxes, and bands filled the air with Latin music, and people gathered in front of their houses for informal meetings and sidewalk parties. While children played stickball and other street games, teenagers and young adults went to dance halls to participate in dance contests and to listen to the jam sessions of competing local bands. Daily wedding processions also added to the color and excitement of El Barrio during the warm summer months.

More than colorful and exciting, El Barrio was, and is, one of the friendliest and most tightly knit communities in

Thousands of Puerto Ricans celebrate their heritage as a Puerto Rican parade passes through the streets of New York City in 1987.

New York. The Puerto Ricans formed warm, lasting friendships in El Barrio, and they usually shared what little they had with their friends and neighbors. No matter how poor they were, the Puerto Ricans never failed to open their doors and their hearts to hungry children and adults.

This warmth and affection was most evident within Puerto Rican families. Puerto Ricans in El Barrio and other Puerto Rican districts on the mainland frequently lived with, or very close to, their relatives. Just as they shared their belongings with their friends and neighbors, so too they shared

whatever they had with their relatives. In many cases, they served as godparents to their brothers' and sisters' children. The godparent system was highly respected, and most Puerto Ricans treated their godchildren just as they treated their own children.

While many traditional nuclear families (single families consisting of a father, mother, and children) fell apart—because of either broken marriages or strained parent-child relations—extended families remained together on the mainland. In fact, problems often strengthened family bonds, bringing relatives closer together.

Despite hardships, family bonds among Puerto Ricans remain strong.

Life for the Puerto Ricans who went to New York and other mainland cities was not easy, but it wasn't all bad either. The jobs were low paying and undesirable, but at least they were jobs. The tenements were old and dingy, but they were better than no homes at all. The cities were cold and forbidding, but friends and family were always there to give warmth and comfort. If life on the mainland was not the best of all possible worlds, neither was it the worst.

4
TOWARD A BETTER LIFE

Girls carry the Puerto Rican flag through the streets of New York City.

Coming Together

During the 1950s and 1960s, more and more Puerto Rican migrants began to look upon themselves as permanent residents of the U.S. mainland. They might still take occasional trips back to Puerto Rico to visit friends and relatives, but they regarded the mainland as their new home. This was especially true of the second-generation Puerto Ricans who were born on the mainland. To many of them, the U.S. mainland was their "heart place," while Puerto Rico remained secondary in their affection.

As the migrants became more certain of their identity—of their status as permanent residents of the mainland—they looked for ways to solve their problems and to improve the quality of their lives. During the mid-1950s, a group of Puerto Ricans living in New York City established

Left: *Raul Vasquez, who learned plumbing through the Job Corps, teaches the trade to other disadvantaged youths.* **Right:** *A meeting of representatives of the National Puerto Rican Forum*

the National Puerto Rican Forum (NPRF), the first major Puerto Rican organization formed on the mainland by the migrants themselves.

The NPRF was organized to give the Puerto Ricans of New York City a voice with which to air their problems and promote their interests. The forum's most important function was to bring the migrants together for the first time, solidifying them as a group. Unified under one organization, New York City's Puerto Rican community was able to attack its problems and fight for improvements with greater power and strength than ever before.

An offshoot of the Puerto Rican Forum was the Puerto Rican Community Development Project. First funded by the U.S. Office of Economic Opportunity in 1965, this militant organization was established to develop specific programs for the improvement of New York City's Puerto Rican community. This organization was instrumental in promoting a sense of identity, stability, and political strength among the Puerto Ricans of New York. Although the project lost its funding in 1979, other organizations continue to provide assistance to the Puerto Rican community through counseling, job training programs, youth organizations, housing projects, and drug rehabilitation programs. The Puerto Rican Family Institute has been instrumental in helping Puerto Rican migrants adjust to life on the mainland.

The Puerto Rican Association for Community Affairs, operates daycare centers, health clinics, bilingual and bicultural educational programs, and other support services for the Puerto Rican community.

Political Awakening

Due partly to the influence of such organizations as the National Puerto Rican Forum and due partly to their growing sense of identity as mainland residents, the Puerto Ricans have made great strides in the area of politics. Before 1965 citizens living in New York and several other mainland cities were required to take a literacy test in English before registering to vote. Spanish had remained the official language of Puerto Rico even after the island's people were made U.S. citizens in 1917. Since many of the Puerto Ricans couldn't read English, they failed the test and were denied the right to vote.

When the Voting Rights Act was passed by Congress in 1965, the discriminatory practice of forcing some voters to take an English literacy test was ended. The law stated that no U.S. citizen who had received an elementary school diploma in a country where the classroom language was other than English could be denied the right to vote. The Voting Rights Act was a great victory for the Puerto Ricans on the mainland, and it allowed many of them to participate in mainland politics and government for the first time.

Today, *"Despierta Borriqua–defiende lo tuyo"* ("Wake up, Puerto Rican –defend what's yours") is a familiar phrase in Puerto Rican communities throughout the United States. The "political awakening" of the Puerto Ricans is reflected by the fact that each year, more and more Puerto Ricans (especially those born on the mainland) are registering to vote. By working "within the system," they are attempting to pass new laws and win new programs that will benefit the Puerto Rican community. Through their political activities, they are also trying to end discriminatory practices in housing, employment, and education.

The growing political awareness and activity of Puerto Ricans has shown in their increased involvement in mainland politics and government. In 1970 the Puerto Ricans living in the Bronx (one of the five boroughs of New York City) displayed their political strength by electing Herman Badillo to the U.S. House of Representatives. A Democrat, Badillo became the first Puerto Rican to be seated in the U.S. Congress. Just as John Kennedy's presidential victory in 1960 removed the prejudice against Catholics in government, Badillo's victory in 1970 helped remove the prejudice against Puerto Ricans in government.

The Young Lords walk in a funeral procession through the streets of El Barrio. They bear the body of a fellow Young Lord who died in prison.

In 1970 New York's Puerto Rican population claimed not only one U.S. Congressman, but also four representatives in the New York state government. By 1987, Puerto Ricans filled 10 offices in New York State, from state representative and state senator to city council member and Bronx borough president.

While most Puerto Ricans have tried to win political and social gains by supporting such conventional, nonviolent organizations as the National Puerto Rican Forum in New York and the Caballeros de San Juan (the Knights of Saint John) in Chicago,

some have supported more radical organizations, such as the Young Lords. This militant organization was established in 1968 by a group of young Puerto Rican radicals in New York's East Harlem district. Patterned after the Black Panthers, the Young Lords demanded "Power to the People." Although the group advocated violence as a means of winning equal rights for the Puerto Rican community (it occupied an East Harlem church in the spring of 1970), it was also involved in many peaceful projects. These projects included youth clubs, drug rehabilitation centers, breakfast programs for ghetto children, and health clinics.

Since the 1950s, many Puerto Rican citizens' groups have been established in New York, Chicago, Boston, and other cities to fight for better housing, education, and employment. In New York, the East Harlem Council for Human Services convinced city officials to tear down some of El Barrio's worst tenements and replace them with modern housing complexes. The council also succeeded in getting new playgrounds, parks, libraries, and health clinics for East Harlem. Another Puerto Rican group, the Emergency Tenants Council (ETC), scored similar successes in Boston. In 1970, ETC organized a strike against a powerful tenement owner and legally forced him to bring his tenements up to city standards. The organization also was involved in a city redevelopment project that began in Boston in 1969.

While such community development projects continued on a local level throughout the 1970s and 1980s, many people saw the need for a *national* voice for the concerns of Puerto Ricans. The National Puerto Rican Coalition, founded in 1977, is composed of representatives from national Puerto Rican associations, prominent local groups, and Puerto Rican businesses. This organization provides a voice for the Puerto Ricans in national affairs and presents the needs and concerns of Puerto Ricans to the nation's lawmakers.

The Puerto Rican Legal Defense and Education Fund was established in 1972 to provide legal assistance to Puerto Ricans and to challenge laws and practices that discriminate against Puerto Ricans in housing, education, and employment. The PRLDEF has won many victories through the courts. Lawsuits have led to the establishment of bilingual assistance for Spanish-speaking voters in New York City and Newark, New Jersey; an end to discriminatory hiring practices in the New York City fire, police, and sanitation departments; and a requirement that Connecticut state welfare offices provide bilingual written material and bilingual social workers.

Education and Jobs

The Puerto Ricans living on the mainland have also made significant progress in the area of education. Aspira of America, the largest and most important educational organization of the Puerto Ricans, was established in New York during the early 1960s. The word *aspira* means "ambition," and Aspira's main goal has been to instill in school-age Puerto Ricans the ambition to finish high school and enter college. Supported by the federal government and by leading Puerto Rican professionals and businesspeople, the organization has set up vocational guidance programs,

Students consider job and educational opportunities at a Career Day sponsored by Aspira of New York.

scholarship funds, English-tutoring programs, and youth clubs in junior and senior high schools throughout the nation.

Another encouraging sign for the Puerto Ricans is the fact that more and more school systems have bilingual education programs for Hispanic, or Spanish-speaking, children. Under these programs, classes are conducted in both English and Spanish. The rise in bilingual education programs for Puerto Rican, Mexican, and Cuban children stems mainly from the federal Bilingual Education Act of 1968. To help "ensure equal educational opportunity to every child," the act has provided school systems with financial aid to start bilingual programs for the "large numbers of children of limited English-speaking ability in the United States." Since the passing of the Bilingual Education Act, bilingual school programs have become the subject of some political controversy. Educators and politicians disagree about ways to implement these programs in the schools. Despite such controversy, however, bilingual programs have been established in many states.

As the Puerto Ricans are becoming better educated, they are finding it easier to get jobs as skilled workers or as professionals. This is especially true of Puerto Ricans who were born on the mainland, many of whom are lawyers, doctors, teachers, social workers, electricians, plumbers, and business owners. Small business owners have received valuable assistance from the Puerto Rican Merchants Association, which at one time counted 5,000 Puerto Rican-owned restaurants, grocery stores, newspapers, laundries, banks, bars, barbershops, and small factories among its membership.

Puerto Rican women in an adult education program. The Job Corps and the U.S. Office of Economic Opportunity have taught many Puerto Ricans new skills and trades.

Many Puerto Rican businesspeople in New York City have received financial assistance from the Small Business Administration—a federal agency that lends money to people who want to establish their own businesses. Two other federal agencies —the U.S. Office of Economic Opportunity and the Job Corps—have helped many Puerto Ricans find work as unskilled or semiskilled laborers. The latter agency has been especially helpful to young Puerto Ricans who have dropped out of school. Through the Job Corps, many of the dropouts have improved their English, earned the equivalent of a high school diploma, and learned a trade.

Although the Puerto Ricans have made important gains in politics, housing, education, and employment, they have not solved all their problems. Many are still unemployed; many are still on welfare; many are still living in the slums; many are still dropping out of school. Yet, in spite of all these problems, the future of the Puerto Ricans in this country looks far brighter than it did 20, or even 10, years ago.

More than 2 million Puerto Ricans are now living on the U.S. mainland. Many have left the central cities and have established their homes, businesses, and community centers in suburban New York, Chicago, Philadelphia, Cleveland, Miami, Hartford, Boston, and other cities throughout the United States. As the Puerto Ricans continue to work together, they continue to make the United States a better place to live—for themselves, and for all Americans.

Puerto Rican students from Chicago attend a meeting sponsored by Aspira of Illinois. Chicago has the second largest Puerto Rican population in the United States.

Major Population Centers of the Puerto Ricans
on the U.S. Mainland, 1990

California
San Francisco 33,700
Los Angeles 62,000

Connecticut
Bridgeport 33,500
Hartford 45,200

Florida
Miami 72,800

Illinois
Chicago 131,400

Massachusetts
Boston 47,100

New Jersey
Camden 23,000

Hoboken 6,800
Jersey City 58,500
Newark 76,800
Paterson 27,600
Perth Amboy 31,900

New York
New York City 933,300
Rochester 21,700

Ohio
Cleveland 21,200

Pennsylvania
Philadelphia 120,000

Wisconsin
Milwaukee 14,500

5
CONTRIBUTIONS TO AMERICAN LIFE

Cellist and conductor Pablo Casals

The Puerto Ricans on the mainland have made important contributions to American life and culture. Many Puerto Ricans have achieved success in government, business, literature and the arts, sports, and entertainment.

Government

Robert Garcia was the first Puerto Rican to be elected to the New York State Senate. Born in New York City's Bronx borough in 1933, Garcia began his career in politics in 1965, when he became the assistant to U.S. Congressional Representative James A. Scheuer. After serving as a congressional assistant for two years, Garcia was elected to the New York State Assembly. Then, in 1968, he ran as

Robert Garcia (left) was the first Puerto Rican elected to the New York State Senate. Herman Badillo (right) was the first Puerto Rican in the U.S. Congress.

a candidate for state senator from New York's East Harlem-South Bronx District. Garcia won in an overwhelming show of strength, becoming New York's first Puerto Rican state senator. In 1978, he was elected to the U.S. House of Representatives, where he served as chair of the Congressional Hispanic Caucus for four years. In 1989 Garcia resigned from Congress after a publicly damaging trial in which he was convicted of extortion.

Like Robert Garcia, Herman Badillo scored another "first." Badillo was the first Puerto Rican to be seated in the U.S. Congress. Unlike Garcia, Herman Badillo is a native of Puerto Rico. He was born in Caguas, a city near San

Juan, in 1929. Badillo came to New York in 1941, shortly after the death of his parents. By working as a dishwasher, he managed to put himself through college and law school. Badillo graduated from the Brooklyn Law School in 1954 and became a practicing lawyer the following year.

Herman Badillo entered politics to further the goals and interests of New York's Puerto Rican community. He received his first major government appointment in 1962, when he was named commissioner of the Department of Relocation. By seeing to it that Puerto Ricans who were moved from the slums were treated fairly and humanely, Badillo won wide support

Maurice Ferré served as mayor of Miami from 1973 to 1985.

in the Puerto Rican community. As a result, he was easily elected in 1965 as president of the Bronx borough—an area that is heavily populated by Puerto Ricans.

Badillo resigned as borough president in 1969 in order to run as a Democratic candidate for mayor of New York City. Although Badillo lost the election to incumbent Mayor John Lindsay, he had considerable support and finished a strong third in the election. When the 1970 elections were held for New York's representatives to the U.S. Congress, Badillo ran as a candidate from New York's 21st congressional district—a district that includes El Barrio. Not surprisingly, Badillo won an easy victory in the election.

As the sole Puerto Rican in the U.S. Congress, Herman Badillo became the most influential political leader of the Puerto Rican community on the mainland. Though defeated in 1978 by Robert Garcia, Badillo remained active in New York politics, becoming deputy mayor for management in 1981. In 1983 he became chair of the Governor's Advisory Committee on Hispanic Affairs. Badillo ran for mayor again in 1991 but later dropped out of the race. He is viewed with respect as a veteran politician.

The nephew of a Puerto Rican statesman, Maurice Ferré was elected mayor of Miami, Florida's largest city, in 1973. Ferré's uncle, Luis A. Ferré, was the governor of Puerto Rico in the late

1960s. Miami has a large number of people of Hispanic origins. The majority of them are Cuban, with a minority of about 73,000 Puerto Ricans. Maurice Ferré was able to form a coalition of these Hispanic voters, along with blacks and whites, to win reelection five times over Cuban and white challengers.

Business

While thousands of Puerto Ricans have established their own businesses on the mainland, others have built successful careers in the corporate world.

John Torres not only established his own business, he also helped hundreds of other merchants build theirs. Born in Puerto Rico, Torres moved to New York City at age 14 and eventually graduated from New York University with a degree in interior design. He gave up his career as a designer in 1960 when he took over a bodega that he had helped his brother buy. Three years later, he founded the Metropolitan Spanish Merchants Association to represent and assist Spanish-speaking merchants. Known as "La Metro," the association represents more than 1,200 small businesses, including restaurants, barbershops, bars, dry cleaners, and bodegas. Torres now heads the Metro Spanish Food Wholesalers, a cooperative formed to supply Hispanic retailers. He also has helped organize businesses and co-operatives in other cities.

Rita DiMartino is the director of international public affairs for AT&T.

As founder of the Metropolitan Spanish Merchants Association, John Torres has helped many Puerto Ricans open and operate small businesses.

Rita DiMartino, director of international public affairs for AT&T

In this job, she represents the interests of the giant communications corporation to the leaders of government and industry in Latin America. She first went to work for AT&T in 1979, after she had been a senior business consultant for the New York State Department of Commerce. DiMartino was born and raised in New York and received a master's degree in public administration from Long Island University. In 1982 President Ronald Reagan appointed her as the U.S. ambassador to the UNICEF executive board. DiMartino also is a nationally recognized spokesperson for the Hispanic community and is active in several important Hispanic organizations.

Literature and the Arts

A number of cultural organizations promoting music, literature, and the arts have been established by the Puerto Ricans living on the U.S. mainland. New York City is home to two of these organizations—the Instituto de Puerto Rico and the Ateneo de Puerto Rico.

Under the guidance of the Instituto de Puerto Rico and the Ateneo de Puerto Rico, several groups of Puerto Ricans have established their own theater companies. One of these, the Puerto Rican Traveling Theater, presents Puerto Rican dramas in the streets of New York each summer. This theater group has been a tremendous success, and it has helped familiarize

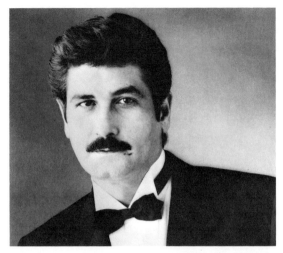

Left: *Novelist, Abraham Rodriguez, Jr., documented Puerto Rican life in the South Bronx.* **Right:** *Opera singer, Justino Díaz*

the Puerto Ricans of New York with the works of such Puerto Rican playwrights as Luis Florens Torres and René Marqués. It celebrated its 20th birthday in April 1987.

Piri Thomas has distinguished himself as a gifted poet and novelist. His most important work has been *Down These Mean Streets*, an autobiographical novel published in 1967. Highly acclaimed by the critics, the best-selling book tells the story of Thomas's life in the ghettoes of East Harlem. Thomas became addicted to drugs as a young man, and much of his hard-hitting book deals with the drug subculture of El Barrio. *Down These Mean Streets* was such a success that in 1968, Harlem-born filmmaker José García turned the book into an award-winning documentary entitled *The*

World of Piri Thomas. Six years later, in 1974, Thomas completed *Seven Long Times*, an autobiographical account of the time he spent behind bars.

Abraham Rodriguez, Jr., is another important Puerto Rican author who achieved national recognition. Raised in the Bronx by a father who instilled in him many dreams of a better life and the desire to write, Rodriguez began writing when he was quite young. His novels and short stories portray the life he has known and seen growing up in the South Bronx and the pain that afflicts the young Puerto Ricans who live there. His first book, *Boy Without a Flag,* and his second, *Spidertown,* provide an important voice for modern young Puerto Ricans straining under the yoke of violence and poverty in their inner-city neighborhoods.

Concert pianist, Jesús Sanromá

Several Puerto Ricans have made significant achievements in the field of classical music. A native of Puerto Rico, bass singer Justino Díaz has sung with the New England Opera Theater, the Opera Company of Boston, the American Opera Society, and the Metropolitan Opera Company, where he became leading bass in 1963.

Like Justino Díaz, concert pianist Jesús María Sanromá was born in Puerto Rico. After moving to the U.S. mainland in 1917, he studied piano at the New England Conservatory of Music. From 1926 to 1943, he was the official pianist of the Boston Symphony. Sanromá gave recitals in London, Paris, Vienna, Madrid, and scores of U.S. cities. He also helped create the Puerto Rico Conservatory. He died in San Juan, in 1984.

Born in Spain, the world-famous cellist and conductor Pablo Casals went to Puerto Rico in 1956 to visit the birthplace of his mother. Casals liked the island so much that he decided to settle there. In 1957 he founded the annual Festival Casals in Puerto Rico. Later, the outstanding musician helped establish the Puerto Rico Symphony Orchestra. After thrilling audiences for three-quarters of a century, Casals died in San Juan in 1973, at the age of 96. "I can never play the same piece twice in the same way," the renowned cellist once said. "Each time it is new."

Sports

Many Puerto Rican athletes have won fame and fortune through their outstanding achievements in sports. In fact, the Puerto Ricans can boast of heroes in such diverse athletic fields as baseball, boxing, horse racing, golf, and tennis.

Several Puerto Ricans have made names for themselves as major league baseball players. During World War II, Hiram Bithorn pitched for the Chicago White Sox and Luis Olmo served as an outfielder for the Brooklyn Dodgers. During the 1950s, Rubén Gómez and Luis "Tite" Arroya pitched for several different National League and American League teams.

Roberto Clemente

Roberto Clemente also came to the mainland and won wide acclaim as a major league player. He was born in Carolina, Puerto Rico, in 1934. After playing professional baseball on the island, Clemente went to the U.S. mainland and joined the Pittsburgh Pirates as an outfielder. During his 18-year career with the Pirates, he won four National League batting titles and 12 Golden Glove Awards for fielding excellence. In 1966, Clemente was named the Most Valuable Player of the

67

Several Puerto Ricans have had notable careers as professional baseball players. They include Orlando Cepeda (above) and Benito Santiago (below).

year. Five years later, he was voted the Most Valuable Player of the World Series. On December 31, 1972, months after becoming the 11th major league player to reach the 3,000-hit mark, Roberto Clemente was killed in a plane crash off the coast of Puerto Rico. (He had been bringing relief supplies to earthquake victims in Nicaragua when the accident occurred.) Three months later, he was elected to the Baseball Hall of Fame.[2]

Island-born Orlando Cepeda also proved himself to be a first-rate baseball player during his 17-year career. The first baseman moved to the U.S. mainland in 1958 to join the San Francisco Giants. At the end of the 1958 season, he was named Rookie of the Year. In 1967, while with the St. Louis Cardinals, Cepeda was voted the National League's Most Valuable Player. He also played with the Atlanta Braves, the Oakland Athletics, and the Boston Red Sox.

In 1987, catcher Benito Santiago of the San Diego Padres had the longest hitting streak ever—32 hits. He batted .346 with 5 home runs and 18 RBIs during his streak. He was named 1987 Rookie of the Year by the National League. He moved to the U.S. mainland in 1982.

[2]The Baseball Writer's Association elected Clemente to the Baseball Hall of Fame on March 20, 1973, waiving the five-year period that ordinarily must elapse between the end of a player's active career and eligibility for the Hall.

In the world of boxing, four Puerto Ricans have been world champions. The first was Sixto Escobar, who became the world bantamweight boxing champion in 1936. He lost the title in 1937, regained it in 1938, and vacated it in 1939. A stadium in San Juan, Puerto Rico, is named after him. Next came José Torres, who won the title of world light-heavyweight boxing champion in 1965. Torres lost the title to Dick Tiger of Nigeria in 1967. During the same year that Torres lost his title, Carlos Ortiz won the title of world lightweight boxing champion—for the fifth time! And in 1987, Wilfredo Vasquez became the world bantamweight boxing champion.

Boxing and baseball are not the only sports in which Puerto Ricans have excelled. Eddie Belmonte won international fame as a prizewinning jockey. The horses he rode earned purses totalling $14 million. Belmonte became a jockey agent after retiring in 1974. Charlíto Pasarell made his mark as an outstanding tennis player in the 1960s. In 1967 Pasarell was ranked number one in the United States. Juan "Chi Chi" Rodríguez is probably better known than Belmonte or Pasarell. Born in Bayamón, Puerto Rico, in 1935, the former caddie became a professional golfer in 1960. Four years later,

Eddie Belmonte

Juan "Chi Chi" Rodríguez

Geraldo Rivera, host of the popular "Geraldo" talk show

Rodríguez was one of the leading tournament winners of the Professional Golf Association. He has represented Puerto Rico in the World Cup Tournament in Singapore. He graduated to the PGA Senior Tour in 1985.

Entertainment

Several individuals of Puerto Rican descent have distinguished themselves in the entertainment world.

Television personalities of Puerto Rican ancestry include Geraldo Rivera and the late Freddie Prinze. A television broadcaster and reporter, Rivera has won many awards, including seven Emmys, a Peabody, and the Associated Press's Broadcaster of the Year. He has worked on such programs as "Good Morning, America" and has hosted his own show, "Geraldo." Freddie Prinze, a comedian-turned-actor, was the son of a Hungarian father and a Puerto Rican mother. He first achieved fame in 1974 by playing the part of a Chicano in the series "Chico and the Man." This show made Freddie Prinze one of the superstars of television comedy in the 1970s. Tragically, Prinze took his own life in 1976.

Dolores Conchita del Rivera shortened her name to Chita Rivera after she became a singing-dancing-acting star of Broadway. The talented performer began taking dancing lessons at age 11, and at 14 she won a scholarship to the School of American Ballet in New York. A few years later,

Rivera landed a featured dancing role in the musical *Call Me Madam*. Major roles in such Broadway musicals as *Can-Can*, *Guys and Dolls*, and *Bye Bye Birdie* followed. One of the star's most memorable parts was as the fiery Anita in the Broadway production of *West Side Story*. She worked with Shirley MacLaine in the 1968 film *Sweet Charity*, and she received the Tony Award for her performance in *The Rink* in 1984.

While Chita Rivera was playing the role of Anita in the Broadway version of *West Side Story*, Puerto Rican actress Rita Moreno (Rosa Dolores Alverio) won fame playing the same role in the film version of the musical. For her performance in the movie, she won an Academy Award as the best supporting actress of 1961. Moreno was born in Humacao, Puerto Rico, in 1931. When she was six, she went to New York with her mother. Two years later, she began singing and dancing at a nightclub in Greenwich Village. At 17 Moreno starred in her first Broadway play, and at 18 she signed a movie contract with Metro-Goldwyn-Mayer. Rita Moreno was in the Guinness Book of World Records as the only performer ever to win all four of the entertainment world's most prestigious awards: the Oscar (1962), the Tony (1975), the Grammy (1972), and the Emmy (1977 and 1978).

Another Puerto Rican Academy Award winner is José Ferrer. Born in Santurce, Puerto Rico, in 1912, the talented actor won the 1950 Oscar

Rita Moreno won an Academy Award for her performance in the film version of **West Side Story.**

for best actor for his moving performance in *Cyrano de Bergerac*. After this success, Ferrer performed in such notable films as *Moulin Rouge*, *The Caine Mutiny*, *Lawrence of Arabia*, and *Ship of Fools*. He starred in the 1966 Broadway hit *The Man of La Mancha*. In 1985, Ferrer received the National Medal of Arts from President Ronald Reagan. Ferrer died in January 1992.

Joining the ranks of successful Puerto Rican actors is Raul Julia. Born in 1940 in San Juan, Puerto Rico, Julia developed his acting career by performing on Broadway and in other New York theaters. He expanded into films, drawing acclaim for his work in *The Eyes of Laura Mars* and *Kiss of the Spider Woman*, which was

nominated for several Academy Awards. He has also appeared in other popular films, including *Tequila Sunrise, Presumed Innocent,* and *The Addams Family*. Julia has remained active on the stage, appearing in a production of *The Winter's Tale* in Shakespeare in the Park and in a remake of *The Man from La Mancha*.

Rosie Perez is another Puerto Rican who has made a name for herself as an actress. She grew up in Brooklyn, a borough of New York City, with 10 brothers and sisters. She had no plans or dreams of becoming an actress. Instead, she worked hard in school, got good grades, and went to college in Los Angeles to become a marine biologist. One night, when she was out dancing

Raul Julia (right) and William Hurt in **Kiss of the Spider Woman**

at a funk reggae club, Spike Lee, the renowned director and actor, spotted her. He thought she would be perfect for the role of Tina, a young Hispanic mother, in his new film *Do The Right Thing.* That film was Perez's big break. She has since appeared in a number of successful films, including *White Men Can't Jump, Night On Earth,* and *Untamed Heart.* She is also the choreographer and sometime dancer for the Fox Television Network's Fly Girls, who appear on "In Living Color."

Menudo was a Puerto Rican singing group that became a hit in the United States in the early 1980s. The group was made up of five Puerto Rican boys aged 13 to 15. Individual group members changed regularly: when a boy reached age 16, he was replaced by a new young singer. Menudo recorded albums in both Spanish and English and made advertisements, television programs, movies, and concert tours throughout the United States. The group was especially popular with teenagers in New York, southern California, Texas, Florida, and other areas with large Hispanic communities.

While the Puerto Rican people have encountered many difficulties in making the transition to the mainland, they have also met with great success. Just as the Puerto Ricans have enjoyed the benefits of life on the mainland, all Americans have benefited from Puerto Rican contributions to government, business, sports, the arts, entertainment, and American culture.

Actress Rosie Perez

INDEX

Puerto Rico Reconstruction Administration, 25
Public Law 600, 29

race relations: on mainland, 36, 43; on Puerto
    Rico, 12, 15, 43, 45, 46
religious life on mainland, 49
Rivera, Chita, 70-71
Rivera, Geraldo, 70
Rodriguez, Abraham, Jr., 65
Rodríguez, Juan "Chi Chi," 69-70
Roosevelt, Franklin D., 24, 25

Sagasta, Práxedes, 19
San Juan, 9, 12-14, 16-17
Sanromá, Jesús María, 66-67
Santiago, Benito, 68
slavery on Puerto Rico, 11, 12, 15, 16, 18
Small Business Administration, 58
Spanish-American War, 20
State Republican Party, 28
storefront churches, 49

Thomas, Piri, 65
Torres, John, 63
Torres, José, 69
Treaty of Paris, 20
Truman, Harry S., 29

United States citizenship, 21, 22, 29, 33, 34, 42
United States Office of Economic Opportunity, 58

Vasquez, Wilfredo, 69
Vilella, Roberto Sánchez, 29
voter registration, 47, 54
Voting Rights Act, 54

welfare programs, 43, 44
West Side Story, 45, 46, 71
women, position in mainland society, 44-45
World War II, 34, 35

Young Lords, 55

ACKNOWLEDGMENTS The photographs in this book are reproduced through the courtesy of: p. 2, Minnesota Hispanic Chamber of Commerce; pp. 6, 18, 28, 29, 30, 31 (bottom), Commonwealth of Puerto Rico, Department of State; p. 8, Environmental Science Services Administration; pp. 10 (top), 15, Institute of Culture, Puerto Rico; p. 10 (bottom), James Ford Bell Library, University of Minnesota; pp. 14, 16, 19, 22, 23, 26, 35, 37 (bottom), 44, 78, Independent Picture Service; p. 12, Rare Books and Manuscripts Division, New York Public Library, Astor, Lenox and Tilden foundations; p. 13, Puerto Rico Department of Tourism; pp. 20, 21, U.S. Signal Corps, National Archives; p. 24, El Mundo; p. 25, Popular Democratic Party; pp. 27, 33, Puerto Rico Urban Renewal and Housing Corporation; pp. 31 (top), 79, Puerto Rico Federal Affairs Administration; p. 32, Wide World Photos; p. 37 (top) United Nations; p. 39, New York Convention and Visitors Bureau; pp. 40, 55, Religious News Service; pp. 41, 42, 48, New York City Housing Authority; pp. 46, 71, Kenneth G. Lawrence's Movie Memorabilia Shop of Hollywood; p. 47, Puerto Rico Tourism Development Corporation; p. 49, United Press International; pp. 50, 52, 77, News World Communication, Inc.; pp. 51, 53, 58, Action; p. 53 (right), National Puerto Rican Forum, Inc.; pp. 57, 59 Aspira; pp. 60, 66, Festival Casals; p. 61 (left), Office of the State Senator, New York; p. 61 (right), Herman Badillo, p. 62, City of Miami; p. 63, John Torres; p. 64, Rita DiMartino; p. 65 (left) Lynette Huang; p. 65 (right), Columbia Artists Management Inc.; p. 67, Pittsburgh Pirates; p. 68 (top), San Francisco Giants; p. 68 (bottom), San Diego Padres Baseball Club; p. 69 (left), New York Racing Association; p. 69 (right), PGA Tour; p. 70, Retna Ltd.; p. 72, Museum of Modern Art/Film Stills Archive; p. 73, Hollywood Book & Poster Co.; p. 74, Agricultural Extension Service, University of Puerto Rico.

Front and back cover photographs are reproduced through the courtesy of Richard B. Levine.

Groups featured in Lerner's In America series:

AMERICAN INDIANS   KOREANS
DANES   LEBANESE
FILIPINOS   MEXICANS
FRENCH   NORWEGIANS
GREEKS   PUERTO RICANS
ITALIANS   SCOTS &
JAPANESE   SCOTCH-IRISH
JEWS   VIETNAMESE

 Lerner Publications Company
241 First Avenue North • Minneapolis, Minnesota 55401